6/20/05   Capstone   21.26

First Facts™

Community Helpers at Work

A Day in the Life of a
Nurse

by Connie Fluet

Consultant:
Ruth D. Corcoran, EdD, RN
Chief Executive Officer
National League for Nursing
New York, New York

Capstone
press

Mankato, Minnesota

First Facts is published by Capstone Press
151 Good Counsel Drive, P.O. Box 669, Mankato, Minnesota 56002
www.capstonepress.com

Library of Congress Cataloging-in-Publication Data
Fluet, Connie.
   A day in the life of a nurse / by Connie Fluet
   p. cm.—(First facts. Community helpers at work)
   Includes bibliographical references and index.
   Contents: How do nurses start their shifts?—What do nurses wear to work?—What do nurses
do?—How do nurses help doctors?—Do nurses take breaks?—What tools do nurses use?—What
skills do nurses need?—How do nurses end their shifts?
   ISBN 0-7368-2631-9 (hardcover)
   1. Nursing—Juvenile literature. [1. Nursing. 2. Occupations.] I. Title. II. Series.
RT61.5.F55 2005
610.73—dc22   2003027839

Editorial credits
Amanda Doering, editor; Jennifer Bergstrom, series designer; Molly Nei, book designer;
   Eric Kudalis, product planning editor

Photo credits
All photographs Capstone Press/Gary Sundermeyer

Artistic effects
Eye Wire, 18; Image Library, 4; PhotoDisc, 13

Capstone Press thanks Alton Waynewood and the Mankato Clinic at Wickersham, Mankato,
   Minnesota, for their assistance in creating this book.

1 2 3 4 5 6 09 08 07 06 05 04

Table of Contents

How do nurses start their shifts?

Nurses have work to do before patients arrive. Nurse Alton begins the morning **shift** at the **clinic**. He gets patients' **charts** ready for the doctor. Alton also fills supplies in the **examination rooms**.

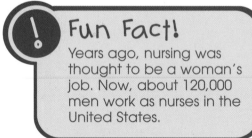

Fun Fact!
Years ago, nursing was thought to be a woman's job. Now, about 120,000 men work as nurses in the United States.

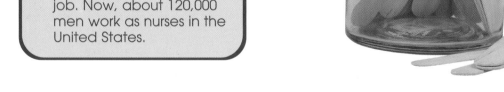

TONGUE DEPRESSORS

8:00 in the morning

5

9:00 in the
morning

6

What do nurses wear to work?

Nurses wear uniforms called scrubs. Scrubs are comfortable shirts and pants. They help keep Alton from spreading **germs**. He also wears clean, comfortable shoes.

Fun Fact!
Female nurses used to wear stiff, white caps and white dresses.

What do nurses do?

Nurses care for patients. Alton welcomes patients as they come in from the waiting room. He asks Wendy how she hurt her hand.

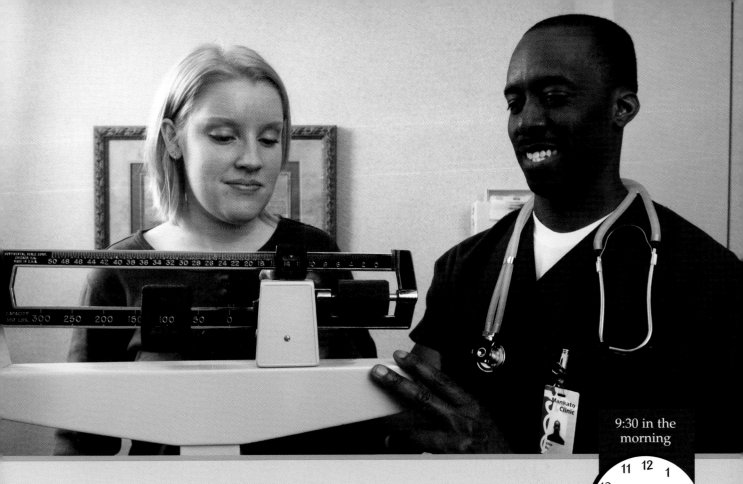

9:30 in the
morning

Nurses also keep records.
Alton measures Wendy's height
and weight. He writes the
measurements on her chart.

How do nurses help doctors?

Nurses help doctors by getting information. Alton takes Wendy's pulse and blood pressure. He asks Wendy questions about how her hand feels. This information helps the doctor find out what is wrong with Wendy's hand.

10:00 in the morning

11

12:00 in the
afternoon

12

Do nurses take breaks?

Nurses take breaks for lunch. They eat in the clinic's break room. Alton has 30 minutes to eat and rest. He eats a salad and a sandwich. These foods help him stay healthy. A good meal gives Alton energy to care for patients.

What tools do nurses use?

Nurses use tools to check a patient's health. Alton uses an ear **thermometer** to measure Jerry's body temperature.

Nurses use other tools. Alton listens to Jerry's heart and lungs with a **stethoscope**. He uses a blood pressure monitor to take Jerry's blood pressure.

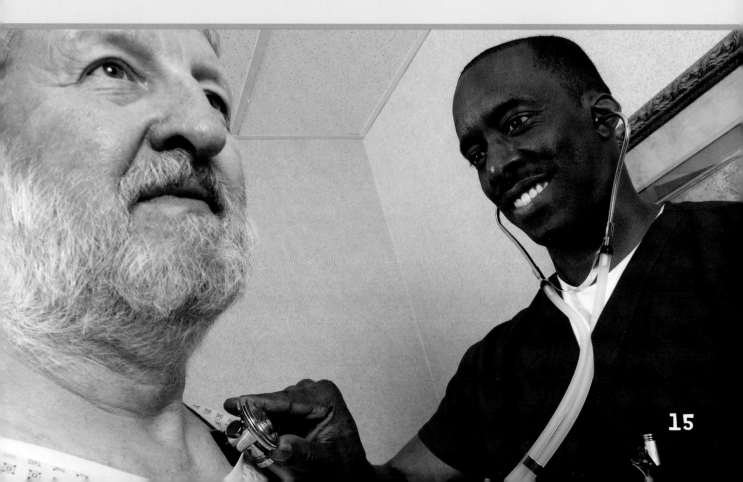

15

What skills do nurses need?

Nurses use many skills. Nurses must like to help people. They help people stay healthy. Alton makes patients feel comfortable at the clinic.

3:00 in the
afternoon

Nurses also use reading and
math skills. Alton reads bottles to
pick out the right medicine. He
uses math to measure how much
medicine to give a patient.

17

How do nurses end their shifts?

Nurses have work to do at the end of their shifts. Alton finishes writing in patients' charts. He writes down the things he did to care for the patients. Alton remembers all of the people he helped today.

Fun Fact!
About 2 million people in the United States work as nurses.

Amazing but True!

Nurses wash their hands before and after touching each patient. They may wash their hands 75 times every day.

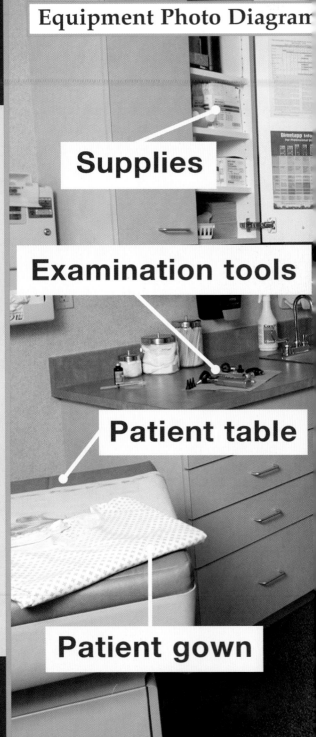

Supplies

Examination tools

Patient table

Patient gown

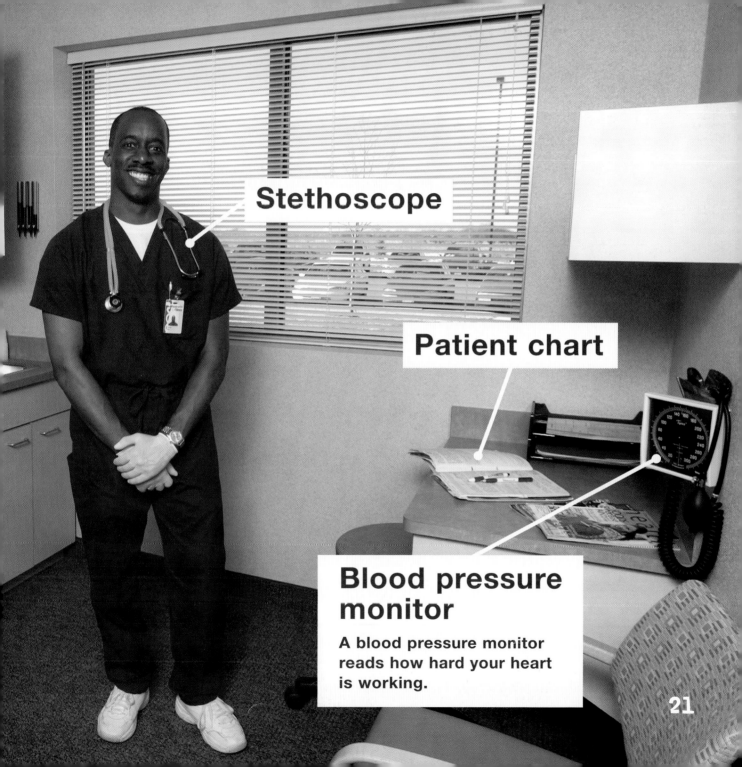

Stethoscope

Patient chart

Blood pressure monitor

A blood pressure monitor reads how hard your heart is working.

Glossary

chart (CHART)—facts kept about a patient's health

clinic (KLIN-ik)—a place people go for medical treatment or advice

examination room (eg-zam-uh-NAY-shuhn ROOM)—the room where a doctor sees patients

germs (JURMS)—small living things that cause diseases

shift (SHIFT)—a set amount of time to work

stethoscope (STETH-uh-skope)—a medical tool used to listen to a patient's heart and lungs

thermometer (thur-MOM-uh-tur)—a tool used to measure body temperature

Read More

Macken, JoAnn Early. *Nurse.* People in My Community. Milwaukee: Weekly Reader Early Learning, 2003.

Miller, Heather. *Nurse.* This is What I Want to Be. Chicago: Heinemann, 2003.

Internet Sites

FactHound offers a safe, fun way to find Internet sites related to this book. All of the sites on FactHound have been researched by our staff.

Here's how:
1. Visit *www.facthound.com*
2. Type in this special code **0736826319** for age-appropriate sites. Or enter a search word related to this book for a more general search.
3. Click on the **Fetch It** button.

FactHound will fetch the best sites for you!

Index